PEOPLE AT
THE CENTER OF

THE CONSTITUTIONAL CONVENTION

By CHRIS HUGHES

BLACKBIRCH PRESS

An imprint of Thomson Gale, a part of The Thomson Corporation

THOMSON

GALE

Detroit • New York • San Francisco • San Diego • New Haven, Conn. • Waterville, Maine • London • Munich

THOMSON
✳
GALE
™

Picture Credits: Cover: background, © Bettmann/CORBIS; lower left, The Corcoran Gallery of Art/COR-BIS; Lower right, © Bettmann/CORBIS; upper left, © Francis G. Mayer/CORBIS; upper right, © Archivo Iconografico,S.A./CORBIS; Art Resource, 31, 34, 36, 39, 41; Bridgeman Art Library, 24; © Archivo Iconografico,S.A./CORBIS, 20; © Bettmann/CORBIS, 5, 9, 11, 12,17, 19, 27, 28, 29, 33, 34, 37; © Corcoran Gallery of Art/CORBIS, 16; © Francis G. Mayer/CORBIS, 15; © Hulton Archive by Getty Images, 23, 26, 35, 38, 40; Mary Evans Picture Library, 30; North Wind Picture Archives, 10, 13, 43; Picture History, 22

LIBRARY OF CONGRESS CATALOGING-IN-PUBLICATION DATA

Hughes, Chris 1968-
  The Constitutional Convention / by Chris Hughes.
    p. cm. — (People at the center of)
  Includes bibliographical references.
  ISBN 1-56711-918-2 (hard cover : alk. paper)
  1. Statesmen—United States—Biography—Juvenile literature. 2. Politicians—United States—Biography—Juvenile literature. 3. United States—Politics and government—1783–1789—Juvenile literature. 4. United States. Constitutional Convention (1787)—Juvenile literature. 5. Constitutional history—United States—Juvenile literature. 6. United States—Politics and government—1775–1783—Juvenile literature. 7. United States—Politics and government—1789–1797—Juvenile literature. I. Title. II. Series.

  E302.5.H84 2005
  973.3'12'0922—dc22

                                                  2004017601

Printed in the United States of America

CONTENTS

THE CONSTITUTIONAL CONVENTION

In 1774, representatives from twelve British colonies in North America gathered in Philadelphia, Pennsylvania. Many colonists were protesting against Britain's treatment of the colonies; they felt the British government was taking advantage of them with unjust taxes and laws. This group of representatives, called the Continental Congress, included men from all of Britain's American colonies except Georgia. They originally met to try to convince Britain to change the most unfair of its laws and taxes, but they had little success. Already, some members were thinking about achieving independence from Britain.

In April 1775, British troops and colonists clashed at the Massachusetts towns of Lexington and Concord. This was the first battle in the American Revolution. In May, the Second Continental Congress was brought together in Philadelphia. (Georgia finally voted to join in July.) Congress appointed George Washington of Virginia as commander in chief of the Continental army. Eventually, Congress also appointed a committee, which included Thomas Jefferson, to explain why the colonies needed to be independent from Britain. In July 1776, Congress signed Jefferson's Declaration of Independence.

Although the British troops were much better armed and trained than the colonists, the distance from Britain and the local soldiers' familiarity with the land helped balance the odds in the war. The Continental army suffered several major losses, including losing control of both New York City and Philadelphia. They also won several battles. Their victory at Saratoga in 1777 finally convinced the French

Members of the Second Continental Congress discuss the Declaration of Independence. The document explains why the colonies desired independence from British rule.

to help their cause, and French troops and money helped the Americans win the war. Washington's troops and their French allies defeated the main British army at Yorktown in 1781, and a final treaty was signed in 1783.

The combined efforts of General Washington and French allies led to an American victory at the Battle of Yorktown in 1781.

The new nation was governed by an agreement called the Articles of Confederation that had been created during the Second Continental Congress. This system gave almost all the governing power to the individual states. There was no single executive in charge of the nation, and any proposal had to be approved by two-thirds of the states, while amendments to the Articles had to be unanimous. It soon became apparent that the government under the Articles of Confederation was too weak to function. The government could not raise money or regulate trade between the states. It did not have enough control over foreign affairs, and it had a limited ability to defend the nation.

In 1786, leaders of Virginia called for all the states to send representatives to Annapolis, Maryland, to discuss some of the weaknesses of the Articles of Confederation. Only five states sent representatives, and those men decided to call for another conference, "to render the constitution of the Federal Government adequate to the exigencies [needs] of the Union,"[1] which would be held in Philadelphia the next summer.

In Massachusetts, another weakness of the government was being exposed. Farmers in western Massachusetts were facing an economic depression. When the state refused to help them, they took arms under the leadership of Daniel Shays and others, and stopped the local courts from meeting. It took several months for Shays' Rebellion to be put down. To many, the economic troubles that led to the rebellion, combined with the inability of the national government to help Massachusetts put down the revolt quickly, further demonstrated the weakness of the Articles of Confederation.

Shays' Rebellion and the call from the Annapolis Convention combined to convince all the states except Rhode Island to send representatives to Philadelphia in May 1787. Fifty-five delegates attended. The initial aim of the conference was to revise the Articles of Confederation, but the group soon decided to discard that model and create an entirely new system. James Madison quickly became the leader of the convention, and his Virginia Plan was one of the first debated. He proposed a bicameral (two-house) legislature in which states were represented based on their population.

That plan was opposed by many of the smaller states, which would have fewer votes because they had smaller populations. William Paterson proposed the New Jersey Plan, with a one-house legislature that gave each state an equal vote. Finally, Roger Sherman presented his Connecticut Compromise, which called for a bicameral legislature in which the Senate would have equal representation and the House of Representatives would have representation based on population. This plan was accepted.

The new system also gave the central government powers that it had lacked under the Articles of Confederation, including the power to tax, regulate trade, and raise and maintain a military. In the end, thirty-nine of the delegates signed the

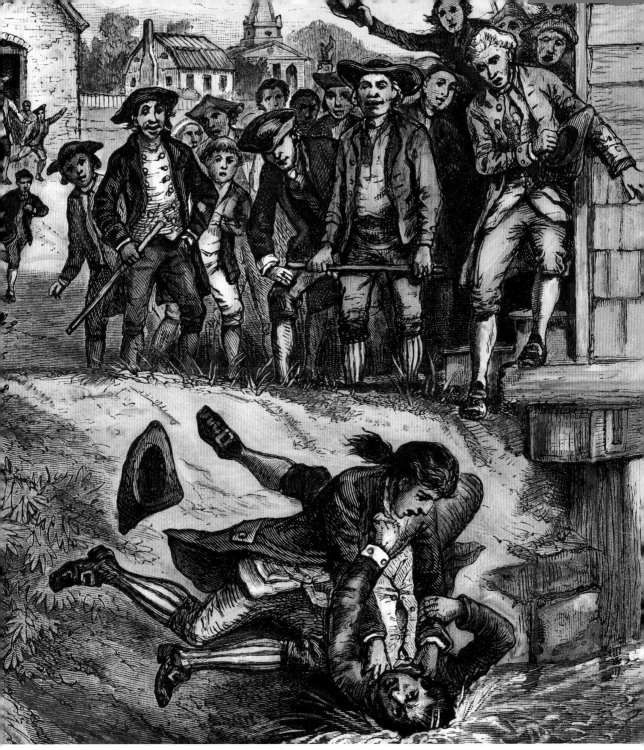

An angry Massachusetts farmer fights with a state official during Shays' Rebellion.

A delegate addresses the Constitutional Convention in 1787. State representatives debated issues of the new Constitution.

new constitution and sent it on to the Continental Congress, which sent it to the states for ratification (approval).

The decision to ratify the Constitution was not an easy one. Those who supported the Constitution were called federalists, and those who opposed it were called antifederalists. Antifederalists thought the Constitution gave too much power to the central government and took too much independence away from the states. In New York, Alexander Hamilton was joined by James Madison and John Jay in writing a series of essays called the Federalist Papers to try to convince people to accept the new government. These essays helped convince people in New York and throughout America to support the Constitution, and eventually all the states ratified the document. In 1789, the new government went into effect, with George Washington as the first president.

The first ten amendments to the Constitution were called the Bill of Rights.

Some states had ratified the Constitution under the condition that certain rights would be added as soon as the government was created. The first ten amendments, passed in 1791, were called the Bill of Rights. Thus was created what has since became the longest-standing written constitution in the world.

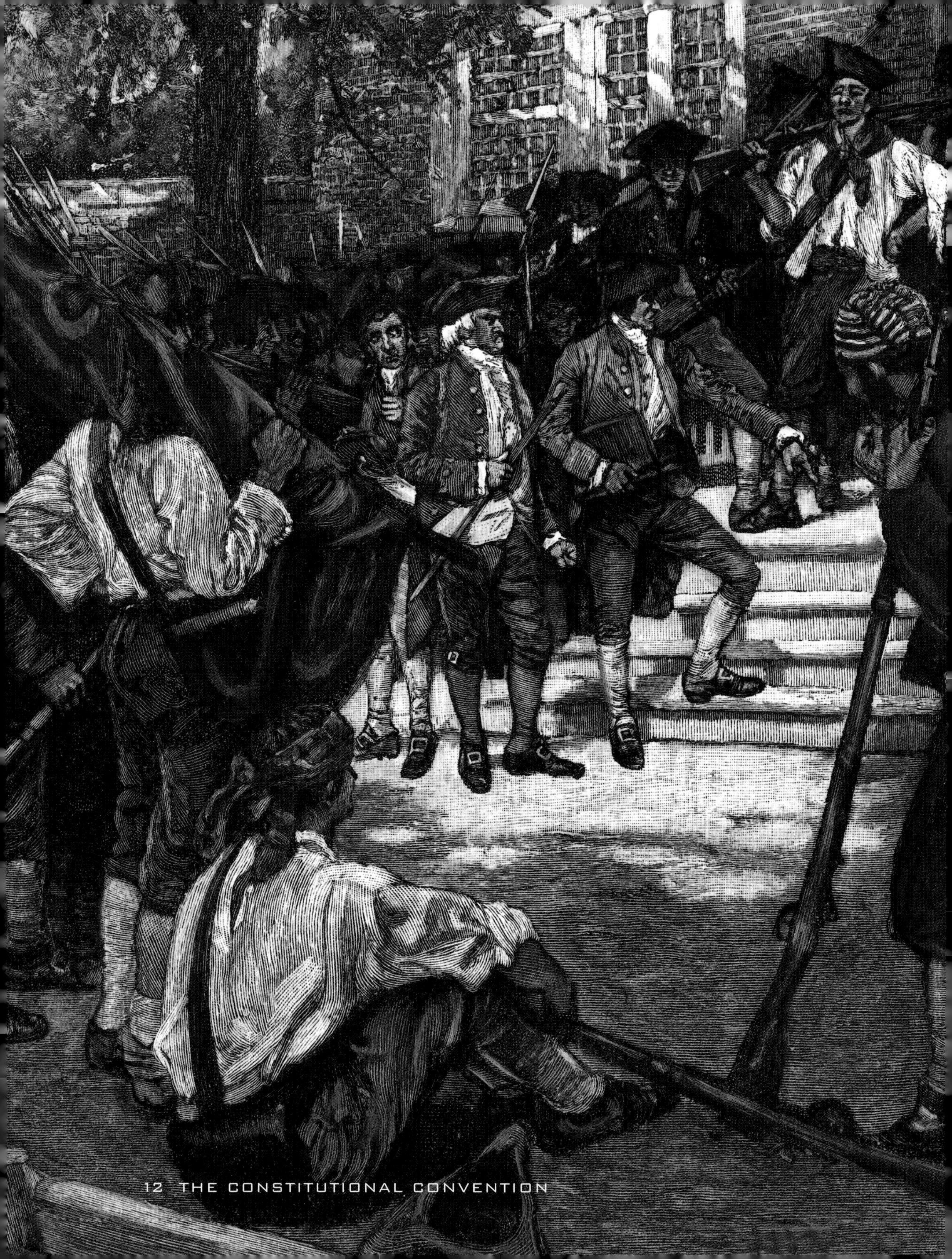

DANIEL SHAYS

LED REBELLION THAT UNDERSCORED NEED FOR
NEW GOVERNMENT

Daniel Shays was born in Hopkinton, Massachusetts, around 1747. Not much is known of Shays' early life. When the Revolutionary War began in 1775, Shays joined the army. He fought in several major battles, including Saratoga, eventually rising to the rank of captain. He was presented with a sword by the Marquis de Lafayette of France in recognition of his bravery and service.

In 1780, Shays resigned from the army and settled in Pelham, Massachusetts. He was a popular figure, and held several public offices. Not long after the war ended, however, America fell into an economic depression that was especially hard on rural areas such as Pelham. Farmers like Shays resented the high taxes they had to pay, and they wanted the state to help them. Instead, the state began taking away property from those who failed to pay, then jailing them. Shays himself was forced to sell the ceremonial sword that Lafayette had given him.

Groups of armed men began forcing the courts to close so that cases against farmers could not be heard. Although there were several leaders of different groups, Shays became the best known, and the entire movement came to be known as Shays' Rebellion. In September 1786, Shays and his followers prevented the state Supreme Court at Springfield from meeting. The following January, Shays led an attack on the federal arsenal at Springfield to obtain weapons for his rebels. This attack failed, and Shays and his men were pursued and defeated on February 4, 1787. Shays himself escaped to Vermont, but the rebellion was over.

The rebellion had sent ripples throughout America. The economic problems that led to the revolt and the inability of the national government to address either the problems or the rebellion highlighted the need for a stronger central government, helped persuade the states to send their representatives to Philadelphia in 1787, and eventually convinced them to ratify the resulting Constitution.

In 1788, Shays asked for a pardon, which was granted. He eventually received a federal pension for his service in the American Revolution. He died in Sparta, New York, in 1825.

Massachusetts farmers, angered that the state will not help them economically, take over a courthouse (opposite). Daniels Shays (right) led the farmers in the revolt known as Shays' Rebellion.

GEORGE WASHINGTON

PRESIDENT OF CONSTITUTIONAL CONVENTIONAL

George Washington was born in 1732 to a landowning family in Virginia. He became a land surveyor at age sixteen and joined the military in 1753. He rose quickly through the militia ranks, fighting for the British during the French and Indian War. From 1759 to 1774, he occupied himself with running his plantation, Mount Vernon, and participating in local government. As resistance to the British increased, Washington's opposition to British policies became stronger, and after fighting broke out in 1775, he was named commander in chief of the Continental army.

After six years of many hardships and defeats, Washington's forces finally defeated the British at Yorktown. In 1783, he resigned from the military and returned to Mount Vernon. Soon, though, Washington realized that America needed a stronger central government, and in 1787, he agreed to attend the Philadelphia Convention, which had been called to revise the Articles of Confederation. Once there, he was unanimously elected president of the convention.

Washington played a vital role in Philadelphia. Although he was not an active speaker at the convention—he made no major speeches at all during the convention—he was so highly respected by the other delegates that he was able to control the proceedings even when tempers flared. In a letter, he explained one of the greatest challenges the convention members had faced: "It is at all times difficult to draw with precision the line between those rights which must be surrendered, and those which may be preserved; and, on the present occasion, the difficulty was increased by a difference among the several States as to their situation, extent, habits, and particular interests."[2] In the end, Washington's connection to the Constitution helped convince many Americans to support it, and he worked hard to make sure Virginia voted to ratify the document.

After the Constitution was ratified, Washington was elected president of the United States. He served two terms, and helped set many of the standards of that office and of the national government. In 1796, he declined a third term in office, and retired to Mount Vernon. He died in 1799, leaving behind a stable government that he had done so much to help establish.

George Washington led his troops to victory at the Battle of Yorktown, was president of the Constitutional Convention, and served as the first U.S. president.

BENJAMIN FRANKLIN

URGED DELEGATES TO SUPPORT CONSTITUTION

Born in Boston in 1706, Benjamin Franklin had very little formal education, but developed a love for reading and learning that eventually led him to a career as a printer, scientist, and inventor. He moved to Philadelphia in 1723, then lived in London for two years before returning to Philadelphia in 1726. Poor Richard's Almanac, which he published, became one of the most popular books in America, and brought him both fame and income.

From 1757 to 1762 and 1764 to 1775, Franklin lived in England, representing several of the colonies and growing more opposed to the British government. In 1775, he returned to the colonies and served in the Continental Congress, helping to draft the Declaration of Independence. Later, in 1776, Franklin returned to Europe, this time as commissioner to France to represent America's interests there. In this rule, he helped to create an alliance between America and France that helped end the war. In 1783, he helped negotiate the Treaty of Paris, which officially ended the Revolutionary War.

After Franklin returned to America in 1785, he was elected president of Pennsylvania, and in 1787, at the age of eighty-one, he was named a delegate to the Philadelphia convention to revise the Articles of Confederation. When the convention was bogged down in a debate between the large states, who supported representation based on population, and the smaller states, who wanted a body based on equal votes,

The oldest of America's Founding Fathers, Benjamin Franklin (opposite) devoted his life to the United States. He helped draw up the Declaration of Independence (above).

Franklin supported the Connecticut Compromise, which created a two-house legislature. He wrote a speech, delivered on the last day of the convention by James Wilson of Pennsylvania because Franklin was too weak, in which he called on all the delegates to support the Constitution. In it, he stated, "I consent, Sir, to this constitution, because I expect no better, and because I am not sure, that it is not the best."[3] Franklin saw very little of the new government; he died in 1790.

JAMES MADISON

Born in 1751 in Virginia, James Madison grew up at his family's estate, Montpelier. He graduated from the College of New Jersey (which would later become Princeton University) in 1771. Although poor health kept him from military service, Madison supported the Revolutionary War as a politician, and he was the youngest delegate to the Continental Congress in 1780. He believed in a strong central government, and after the war, he pushed for a convention to revise the Articles of Confederation. When the Annapolis Convention failed in 1786, Madison helped organize the Philadelphia Convention the following year.

Madison quickly became a leader of the proceedings. As Georgia delegate William Pierce described, "In the management of every great question [Madison] . . . took the lead in the Convention."[4] Madison was the third most frequent speaker at the conference, making more than 150 speeches. His Virginia Plan, presented by fellow Virginian Edmund Randolph, was the starting point for the convention. It called for a bicameral legislature, with a single chief executive and a judiciary, and a system of checks and balances that would protect any branch from becoming too powerful. His plan called for representation in both houses of Congress to be based on population. This was opposed by the smaller states, but eventually a compromise was reached in which one house would have equal representation and the other would have representation based on population.

The final Constitution contained many of Madison's main concepts, and he is often called the "father of the Constitution." After the Constitution was sent to the states for ratification, Madison worked hard to see that it was approved. He joined Alexander Hamilton and John Jay in writing a series of essays, called the Federalist Papers, that explained why this government was necessary. He also actively debated within Virginia to win approval of the Constitution.

When the new government was established, Madison served in the House of Representatives from 1789 to 1797, where he helped sponsor the first ten amendments to the Constitution, called the Bill of Rights. He was appointed secretary of state by Thomas Jefferson in 1801, and in 1809, he succeeded Jefferson as president. Madison was in office during the War of 1812 against Britain. He retired to Montpelier in 1817, and lived there until his death in 1836. His journal of the Constitutional Convention, the best record of that event, was published by the government in 1840.

Called the "father of the Constitution," James Madison contributed many ideas to the document and worked for its approval.

ALEXANDER HAMILTON

HELPED CONVINCE NEW YORK TO RATIFY CONSTITUTION

Born in the West Indies in 1757 (or 1755; the exact year is not certain), Alexander Hamilton was educated in New York City at what would later become Columbia University. He favored independence from Britain, fighting in several battles throughout 1776–1777. In 1777, he joined Gen. George Washington's staff, then left again to lead troops at Yorktown in 1781.

After the war, Hamilton was elected to the Continental Congress in 1782. An advocate for a strong federal government, Hamilton represented New York at the Annapolis Convention, called to discuss strengthening the Articles of Confederation, in 1786. When that conference failed to attract enough supporters, Hamilton helped push for a conference in Philadelphia in 1787.

In Philadelphia, Hamilton called for a stronger central government than most of the delegates wanted. In fact, he proposed that the president and senators should serve in office for life. His views were too strong for most, and Hamilton actually was absent for much of the convention. He returned for the end of the convention, and although the end result was not as strong as he hoped, he was the only representative from New York to sign the Constitution.

Once the Constitution was finished, it had to be ratified by the states. Hamilton, along with fellow New Yorker John Jay and James Madison of Virginia, wrote a series of essays called the Federalist Papers. These eighty-five essays, all written anonymously under the penname Publius, were designed to convince people of the benefits of the proposed government under the Constitution. The Federalist Papers have also served to help explain the meaning and intent behind various parts of the Constitution. Hamilton wrote approximately fifty-two of these essays, and his writing and speeches helped convince New York to ratify the Constitution in 1788.

In the new government created in 1789, Washington made Hamilton the first secretary of the treasury. In that post he helped organize and establish the government's finances. Hamilton opposed another New York politician named Aaron Burr in his bid for the presidency in 1800, and again in Burr's attempt to become governor of New York in 1804. Later that year, Burr challenged Hamilton to a duel. On July 11, 1804, Burr shot Hamilton, who died the next day.

Alexander Hamilton helped write a series of essays called the Federalist Papers, which promoted the proposed constitutional government.

JOHN JAY

COAUTHOR OF THE FEDERALIST PAPERS

Born to a wealthy family in New York City in 1745, John Jay attended King's College (which later became Columbia University). He studied law, and opened his own law office in 1771. In the years leading to the American Revolution, Jay became involved in politics. He tried to maintain a middle path between the radicals who wanted immediate independence and the loyalists who wanted to remain a part of Britain. He served on the Continental Congress from 1774 to 1776.

From 1776 to 1777, Jay helped write New York's state constitution, and in 1777, he was appointed chief justice of New York's Supreme Court. The next year, he

John Jay (opposite) helped negotiate the Treaty of Paris (above). Later he worked to have America's Constitution formally approved at the New York ratification convention.

returned to the Continental Congress, this time to serve as its president. In 1780, Jay was sent to Spain to seek a strong alliance and financial support for America. For the most part, he was unsuccessful, and in 1782 he joined his fellow Americans Benjamin Franklin and John Adams in France. Together they negotiated the Treaty of Paris in 1783, which officially ended the Revolutionary War. Upon his return home in 1784, Jay became America's secretary for foreign affairs, a post he held until 1789.

Jay supported the development of a strong central government, which the nation did not have under the Articles of Confederation. Although he was not selected to attend the Philadelphia Convention, he was one of the most important figures in the country in the quest to have the new Constitution ratified. Jay joined fellow New Yorker Alexander Hamilton and Virginian James Madison to write a series of essays called the Federalist Papers. Jay wrote five of these essays, which were printed in newspapers throughout the country and helped convince people to support the Constitution. Jay was also instrumental in New York's ratification convention, writing a pamphlet called "An Address to the People of New York" that helped win the vote for ratification.

When the new government was established in 1789, George Washington selected Jay as the nation's first Chief Justice of the Supreme Court, a post he held until 1795. That year, Jay was elected governor of New York; he served two terms before retiring in 1801. He died in 1829 at the age of eighty-three.

JOHN DICKINSON

John Dickinson was born to a prominent family in Maryland in 1732; they moved to Delaware when John was eight years old. He was educated by private tutors until 1750, when he went to Philadelphia to study law. From 1753 to 1757, he continued his education in England before returning to Philadelphia to practice law.

In 1760, Dickinson served in the Delaware assembly, and in 1762 he was elected to the assembly in Pennsylvania. As the tension rose between Britain and America, Dickinson wrote a series of letters called "Letters from a Farmer in Pennsylvania," which were published in newspapers. These letters described how the actions of the British were in opposition to Britain's stated ideals of rights and freedoms.

At first, Dickinson hoped to end the troubles between Britain and the colonies without a revolution. As a member of the Continental Congress, he refused to sign the Declaration of Independence. At the same time, he led the effort to create the Articles of Confederation, which laid out the new government. He was voted out of Congress by Pennsylvanians in 1776, and declined reelection in Delaware. He briefly enrolled in the army, but saw very limited action during the war. He served as president of Delaware for one year, in 1781.

Dickinson returned to Pennsylvania, and served as its president from 1782 to 1785. In 1786 he represented Delaware at the Annapolis Convention, called to revise the Articles of Confederation, and was elected president of the convention. However, a lack of support from a majority of states forced the members to agree to meet the next year in Philadelphia. There, his political skills helped shape the Constitution. When large states and small states were at an impasse regarding representation in Congress, Dickinson helped put together the Connecticut Compromise, which was designed to satisfy both sides. Once home, he again put his pen to good use, writing several public letters supporting ratification under the pen name Fabius. In 1787, Delaware became the first state to ratify the Constitution.

Dickinson retired after the convention. He was known as "the penman of the Revolution" for his letters before, during, and after the war. He also gave his support and his name to Dickinson College in Pennsylvania. John Dickinson died in Delaware in 1808.

John Dickinson helped settle the issue of states' representation by working on the Connecticut Compromise at the Philadelphia convention.

EDMUND RANDOLPH

HELPED CONVINCE VIRGINIA TO RATIFY CONSTITUTION

Born in Williamsburg, Virginia, in 1753, Edmund Randolph was a part of a powerful and influential family. He attended the College of William and Mary, and studied law with his father. When the Revolutionary War began, Randolph's father remained loyal to the British and returned to England. Edmund joined the revolutionaries, serving on Gen. George Washington's staff in 1775. In 1776, Randolph left the military and began his career in politics.

He was the youngest member at the convention at which Virginia created its constitution in 1776, and he later served as mayor of Williamsburg, as attorney general for Virginia, and as governor of Virginia from 1786 to 1789. In 1786, Randolph was selected to attend the Annapolis Convention, called to revise the Articles of Confederation, and he was sent to the Philadelphia Convention the next year. In Philadelphia, he presented the Virginia Plan, which was designed mostly by fellow Virginian James Madison. This plan called for two houses of Congress in which states were represented based on population, which favored large states such as Virginia.

Although the final Constitution called for one house with representation based on population and another house with equal votes for every state, many features of the Virginia Plan were a part of the document. Randolph, however, chose not to support the Constitution, and refused to sign it. He feared the power given to the executive branch; he did not want so much power invested in any individual. He thought there should be another convention to work out some of the remaining flaws.

When it came time to ratify the Constitution, however, Madison convinced Randolph to reverse his position, and together they were able to get Virginia to ratify the document. In the new government under Washington, Randolph served as attorney general from 1789 to 1794, and as secretary of state from 1794 to 1795. He retired in 1795, later writing a history of Virginia, and he died in 1813.

Randolph (above, far right) served as attorney general in President George Washington's cabinet.
Edmund Randolph (left) refused to sign the Constitution even though it contained many features of the Virginia Plan.

WILLIAM PATERSON

PRESENTED NEW JERSEY PLAN

Born in Ireland in 1745, William Paterson moved with his family to America in 1747. William's father found a home and success in New Jersey, and William attended the College of New Jersey (now Princeton University). Paterson became a lawyer, and as difficulties with Britain grew, he became highly involved in New Jersey politics. From 1776 to 1783, he was New Jersey's attorney general.

Paterson stayed out of politics for several years after 1783, until he was selected to attend the Philadelphia Convention

The Constitutional Convention was held in the State House in Philadelphia (above).

in 1787. Once there, he realized that the Virginia Plan for the new government would favor the large, highly populated states over the smaller states, including New Jersey. In opposition, Paterson submitted the New Jersey Plan. This plan called for a single house of legislature in which each state would have an equal vote. The final Constitution included parts of both the Virginia and the New Jersey plans: The Senate, in which all states have the same number of votes, is a result of Paterson's efforts.

When the Constitution was ratified and the new government created, Paterson was elected to the Senate that he had helped design. He served in the Senate from 1789 to 1790; from 1790 to 1793 he was governor of New Jersey; and from 1793 to 1806 he was an associate justice on the U.S. Supreme Court. He died in New York in 1806.

William Paterson (opposite) introduced the New Jersey Plan at the convention. The plan proposed a single house of legislature that had equal state representation.

GOUVERNEUR MORRIS

WROTE MOST OF FINAL CONSTITUTION

Born to a wealthy New York family in 1752, Gouverneur Morris showed signs of exceptional intelligence at a very early age. He was educated by private tutors and graduated from what would later become Columbia University at age sixteen, then studied law and became a lawyer by age nineteen. As the Revolutionary War loomed, Morris sided with the rebels, and with his half brother, Lewis, who signed the Declaration of Independence. Despite having lost his right leg in an accident when he was young, Morris served in the militia; however, he soon discovered that he was far more effective as a politician than as a soldier.

A keen politician and statesman, Gouverneur Morris (opposite) wrote most of the Constitution. Even though Morris (above) had lost a leg as a young man, he joined the militia during the Revolutionary War.

A member of New York's State legislature, Morris helped draft the state constitution in 1776, and he joined the Continental Congress in 1778. In 1779, Morris was voted out of Congress; he moved to Philadelphia, and in 1787 he was selected to attend the Constitutional Convention as a representative of Pennsylvania. There, he was among the most important leaders at the conference. He made 173 speeches, more than any other delegate, and supported the movement to create a strong central government. Morris believed that "in all Communities there must be one supreme power, and one only."[5] Most importantly, as a member of the Committee on Style, Morris actually wrote the preamble and most of the final document.

In 1790, George Washington sent Morris to London to attempt to work out remaining problems with Britain, and in 1792, Washington appointed Morris minister to France. He served in that position for two years, and remained in Europe until 1799. He served in the Senate from 1800 to 1803. Afterward, he remained involved with politics, chairing the Erie Canal Commission from 1810 to 1813. He died in 1816.

GEORGE MASON

George Mason was born in Virginia in 1725. His father died when George was ten years old, and the boy moved in with an uncle. He eventually became a lawyer and was one of the wealthiest men in Virginia.

As a businessman, Mason found himself affected by the acts and taxes of Britain, and soon became a leader of the movement toward independence. In 1776, as a member of Virginia's legislature, he wrote Virginia's Declaration of Rights. This document was used as a model by several other states, and by fellow Virginian Thomas Jefferson when he wrote the Declaration of Independence later that same year.

Mason spent several years out of politics beginning in 1780. He was selected to attend the Annapolis Convention in 1786 to discuss revisions to the Articles of Confederation, but chose not to attend. In 1787, however, he attended the Constitutional Convention in Philadelphia, and he was among the most frequent speakers there. By the end of the convention, though, Mason decided not to support the Constitution. He wrote out a series of objections to the document, and distributed them to his peers at the convention. Among other things, he feared that the government the Constitution established would be too powerful; he wanted the rights of individual citizens to be a part of the document. He refused to sign the Constitution, and attempted—but failed—to keep Virginia from ratifying it.

After the Constitution was ratified, a set of ten amendments, called the Bill of Rights, was added. These were the rights Mason supported; in fact,

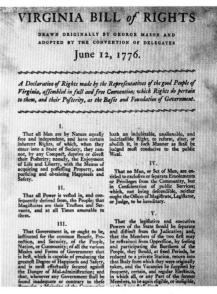

George Mason (opposite) was the guiding force behind the Virginia Bill of Rights (above), which influenced the creation of the Constitution's Bill of Rights. He worried that the government would have too much power and refused to sign the Constitution.

they were modeled after the Declaration of Rights he had written for Virginia in 1776. With these amendments added and some additional limits placed on the federal courts, Mason came to accept the Constitution. He never returned to public office, however, and died at his Virginia estate in 1792.

CHARLES PINCKNEY

Charles Pinckney was born in Charleston, South Carolina, in 1757. The son of a wealthy lawyer, he was educated by private tutors, and became a lawyer himself. During the Revolutionary War, he served in the Continental Congress from 1777 to 1778, and in 1779 he joined the military. Captured by the British in 1780, Pinckney was released the following year. In 1784, he returned to the Continental Congress, where he served until 1787. In 1786, he submitted a recommendation that the Articles of Confederation should be amended to strengthen the national government. Under the articles, the states had to agree unanimously to any changes, however, and his motion failed. Later that year, five states sent their delegates to Annapolis to debate the same topic, and the next year, Pinckney represented South Carolina at the Constitutional Convention.

Charles Pinckney (opposite) and his cousin Charles Cotesworth Pinckney (above) signed the Constitution and pressed South Carolina to ratify it.

Pinckney was one of the youngest delegates at the convention, and one of the most vocal. He spoke often and strongly in favor of a strong central government and was influential in the development and wording of parts of the final document. Pinckney signed the Constitution along with his cousin Charles Cotesworth Pinckney, who also represented South Carolina. Together, they pushed South Carolina to ratify the Constitution. Years after the convention, Pinckney claimed that he had submitted a draft that was the primary basis for the final Constitution, but this claim has been discarded by most historians.

In 1789, Pinckney was elected governor of South Carolina, a post he held three times, from 1789 to 1792, 1796 to 1798, and 1806 to 1808. In 1798, he became a member of the Senate, and from 1801 to 1804 he served as minister to Spain. In 1818, he made a final entry into national politics, serving in the House of Representatives until 1821, when failing health forced him to retire. Pinckney died in 1824.

JAMES WILSON

Born in 1742 in Scotland, James Wilson attended several of the finest universities in Scotland, though he did not earn a degree before coming to America in 1765. He arrived near the height of the tensions between the Americans and Britain. He moved to Pennsylvania, where he taught Latin, and learned law under John Dickinson.

Wilson quickly became involved in the conflict with Britain, and rose to the heights of the Pennsylvania political world. From 1775 to 1777, he served in the Continental Congress, and in 1776 he signed the Declaration of Independence. He returned to Congress from 1782 to 1783 and 1785 to 1787.

In 1787, Wilson was one of Pennsylvania's delegates to the Constitutional Convention in Philadelphia. There, he quickly became one of the most influential and outspoken delegates. His speeches numbered second only to fellow Pennsylvanian Gouverneur Morris, and some said that his influence was greater than anyone aside from James Madison of Virginia. He believed strongly in the idea of a

Pennsylvania delegate James Wilson (opposite) had great influence at the Constitutional Convention (above). He believed the president should be elected directly.

powerful executive, and was one of few delegates to support the idea of the direct election of the president. He asked his fellow delegates, "Can we forget for whom we are forming a Government? Is it for men, or for the imaginary beings called States?"[6] After the convention, Wilson pushed Pennsylvania to ratify the Constitution. Wilson then helped write Pennsylvania's state constitution.

Under the new government in 1789, Wilson became an associate justice on the U.S. Supreme Court. He also became the first professor of law at the University of Pennsylvania. While serving as a Supreme Court justice, he made several bad financial investments, and fell so far into debt that he even spent some time in prison. He remained on the Supreme Court until his death in 1798.

ROGER SHERMAN

INTRODUCED CONNECTICUT COMPROMISE

Roger Sherman was born in Massachusetts in 1721. He showed great interest in learning; since his family had little money to send him to school, he educated himself by reading as much as possible. In 1743, Sherman moved to Connecticut, where he became a successful merchant and surveyor. He took up the study of law, and, still without any formal education, he became a lawyer in 1754.

Sherman was elected to the Connecticut Assembly in 1755, and he also served as a judge and published several essays. From 1774 to 1781 and 1783 to 1784,

Roger Sherman (opposite) helped draft the Declaration of Independence (above). He later developed the Connecticut Compromise, the solution to equal representation for states.

Sherman represented Connecticut in the Continental Congress. There, he was a member of the committee that drafted the Declaration of Independence, and, later, the committee that wrote the Articles of Confederation. At the same time, he was serving as a member of Connecticut's Superior Court, and in 1784 he was elected mayor of New Haven.

In 1787, Sherman continued his public service by attending the Philadelphia Convention. As a representative of a smaller state, he resisted the Virginia Plan, which would establish a state's representation in Congress based on its population. Sherman helped develop the small states' response, called the New Jersey Plan, which called for each state to have an equal vote. Most importantly, when those two plans stalled, Sherman developed the Connecticut Compromise (also called the Great Compromise), which established two houses of Congress, one with equal votes and one with votes based on population. That compromise helped move the convention forward and allowed the Constitution to be completed.

After the convention, Sherman wrote a series of anonymous essays published in Connecticut newspapers, helping to gain support for the Constitution. When the new government was established, Sherman served in the House of Representatives from 1789 to 1791 and the Senate from 1791 until his death in 1793.

Richard Henry Lee was born in Virginia in 1732, to a family of great wealth and influence. Lee was educated in England before returning to America as a young man. He became a justice of the peace in Virginia in 1757, and joined the Virginia legislature in 1758.

In 1774, Lee joined the Continental Congress, and it was his proposal that led to the creation of the Declaration of Independence. In fact, had Lee not been called home because of illness in his family, he would have been chosen to write the Declaration instead of Thomas Jefferson. Lee served in Congress until his own poor health forced him home in 1779. He then served in the Virginia legislature until 1784, when he returned to Congress, this time as president of Congress.

Richard Henry Lee (opposite) worried that central government would become too powerful, and he opposed the Constitution until the Bill of Rights was adopted (above).

When the call came for the states to send delegates to Philadelphia in 1787, Lee refused to attend. He knew that the delegates would work to strengthen the central government, and he feared that the states would lose the freedoms they had fought for in the Revolutionary War. He opposed the conference, and when the Constitution was written, he tried to keep it from being ratified. The lack of a Bill of Rights seemed to confirm to Lee that the government would have too much power. A series of letters arguing against the Constitution, mailed to newspapers under the pen name The Federal Farmer, may have been written by Lee; certainly he was active in his opposition to the proposed government.

In spite of Lee's work, the Constitution was ratified and the new government established. Lee's stand did not cost him popularity however; he was chosen to serve as one of Virginia's first senators in 1789. In that role, he was able to push forward the Bill of Rights that he felt was so necessary, especially the Tenth Amendment, which ensures that any powers not given to the federal government are reserved for the states or for the people. These amendments made Lee much more comfortable with the new government. Lee served in the Senate until 1792, when his health again forced his resignation. He died at home in 1794.

1764	Organized colonial resistance to British acts begins.
September 1774	The First Continental Congress is formed in Philadelphia. Georgia chooses not to attend.
April 1775	The Battles of Lexington and Concord signal the beginning of the American Revolution.
May 1775	The Second Continental Congress convenes in Philadelphia.
May 1776	Congress authorizes the colonies to write their own constitutions.
July 1776	Congress approves and signs the Declaration of Independence.
September 1776	The British capture New York City.
September 1777	The British capture Philadelphia.
October 1777	The Americans defeat the British at Saratoga, New York.
November 1777	Congress adopts the Articles of Confederation.
February 1778	An alliance is created between America and France.
October 1781	American and French forces defeat the main British army at Yorktown, Virginia.
September 1783	The Treaty of Paris is signed, officially the ending war. It is ratified by Congress in January 1784.
September 1786	Shays' Rebellion begins in Massachusetts in response to economic depression.
September 1786	A convention is held in Annapolis to revise the Articles of Confederation. Only five states attend.

George Washington moderates the debate at the Constitutional Convention in Philadelphia. The Constitution remains a viable document.

May 1787	The convention in Philadelphia begins. Delegates discard the Articles of Confederation and write a new Constitution.
September 1787	Congress submits the Constitution to states for ratification.
December 1787	Delaware becomes the first state to ratify the Constitution.
June 1788	New Hampshire becomes the ninth state to ratify Constitution, making it official.
February 1789	George Washington becomes the first president of the United States under the Constitution.

FOR FURTHER INFORMATION

BOOKS

Catherine Drinker Bowen, *Miracle at Philadelphia: The Story of the Constitutional Convention*, May to September, 1787. Boston: Little, Brown, 1986.

Mary E. Hull, *Shays' Rebellion and the Constitution in American History*. Berkeley Heights, NJ: Enslow, 2000.

Marilyn Prolman, *The Constitution*. Chicago: Children's Press, 1995.

Barbara Silberdick Feinberg, *The Dictionary of the U.S. Constitution*. New York: Franklin Watts, 1999.

Gail Stewart, *The American Revolution*. San Diego: Blackbirch Press, 2003.

WEB SITES

Documents in Law, History, and Diplomacy, The Avalon Project at Yale Law School
www.yale.edu/lawweb/avalon/avalon.htm
Includes James Madison's notes on the debates at the Constitutional Convention (www.yale.edu/lawweb/avalon/debates/debcont.htm).

Colonial Hall
www.colonialhall.com/index.php
Biographies of Founding Fathers and the wives of several of the signers of the Constitution.

Congressional Biographical Directory
http://bioguide.congress.gov
Biographical sketches of all people who have served in Congress.

Documents from the Continental Congress and the Constitutional Convention, Library of Congress
http://memory.loc.gov/ammem/bdsds/bdsdhome.html
Major collection of documents relating to Congress and the Constitutional Convention of 1787, a timeline, and a bibliography.

FOR FURTHER INFORMATION

Charters of Freedom, National Archives
www.archives.gov/national_archives_experience/charters/charters.html
Major research site on the Declaration of Independence, the Constitution, and the
Bill of Rights, including biographical sketches.

National Constitution Center
www.constitutioncenter.org/explore/TheU.S.Constitution/index.shtml.
Text of the Constitution, fast facts, biographies, and links.

NOTES

1. The Report of the Annapolis Conference, September 14, 1786, The U.S. Constitution Online. www.usconstitution.net/annapolis.html.

2. Letter from George Washington to the Confederation Congress, accompanying the Constitution, September 17, 1787, quoted in The Debates and Proceedings in the Congress of the United States, vol. 1. www.memory.loc.gov/ammem/amlaw/ac001/intro3.html.

3. Speech of Benjamin Franklin, delivered at the Constitutional Convention September 17, 1787; The U.S. Constitution Online. www.usconstitution.net/franklin.html.

4. "Notes of Major William Pierce (Georgia) in the Federal Convention of 1787," Avalon Project at Yale Law School. www.yale.edu/lawweb/avalon/const/pierce.htm.

5. Quoted in James Madison, Journal on the Debates in the Federal Convention of 1787, May 30, 1787, The Constitution Society. www.constitution.org/dfc/dfc_0530.htm.

6. Quoted in James Madison, Journal on the Debates in the Federal Convention of 1787, June 30, 1787, The Constitution Society. www.constitution.org/dfc/dfc_0630.htm.

INDEX

ABOUT THE AUTHOR

Chris Hughes holds a B.A. in history from Lafayette College and an M.A. in social studies education from Lehigh University. A history teacher and school administrator, Hughes teaches both U.S. and world history and has written several books on the American Civil War and on developing nations. Hughes currently lives and works at a boarding school in Chatham, Virginia, with his wife, Farida, and their children, Jordan and Leah.